DRESSING A NATION
THE HISTORY OF U.S. FASHION

THE LITTLE
BLACK DRESS
and ZOOT
SUITS

Depression and Wartime

FASHIONS
from the
1930s
to the
1950s

ALISON MARIE BEHNKE

TFCB

TWENTY-FIRST CENTURY BOOKS
MINNEAPOLIS

Dedication

To Audrey, to Marlene, to Kate and to Liz; to all the women who have so ably demonstrated over the decades that true style is an art, and is about a great deal more than the clothes (while also making it clear that great clothes, worn with elegance and intelligence, can truly be works of art).

Cover image: Actress Martha Hyer wears a little black dress and wide-brimmed hat in 1955.

Back cover image: Eddie "Rochester" Anderson wears a zoot suit for his appearance in the musical film *Star Spangled Rhythm* in 1942.

Image on facing page: Actress Audrey Hepburn wears a little black dress in 1952.

Twenty-First Century Books
A division of Lerner Publishing Group, Inc.
241 First Avenue North
Minneapolis, MN 55401 U.S.A.

Website address: www.lernerbooks.com

Library of Congress Cataloging-in-Publication Data

Behnke, Alison Marie.
    The little black dress and zoot suits : Depression and wartime fashions from the 1930s to the 1950s / by Alison Marie Behnke.
        p.   cm. — (Dressing a nation: the history of U.S. fashion)
    Includes bibliographical references and index.
    ISBN 978–0–7613–5892–3 (lib. bdg. : alk. paper)
    1. Fashion—United States—History—20th century—Juvenile literature. 2. Clothing and dress—United States—History—20th century—Juvenile literature. 3. United States—Social life and customs—20th century—Juvenile literature. I. Title. II. Title: Depression and wartime fashions from the 1930s to the 1950s.
    GT615.B45 2012
    391.00973—dc22   2010035444

Manufactured in the United States of America
1 – MG – 7/15/11

CONTENTS

Chapter One

WOMEN'S EVERYDAY WEAR

The 1920s were an era of optimism, parties, and excess. Young people, in particular, rebelled against the strict social rules of earlier times, and the era brought new freedom for women. The fashions of the twenties had reflected these changes. For example, the hemlines of women's dresses rose higher than in previous years. Most women wore dresses that fell to mid-calf, but the most daring showed off their knees. Women also began to wear their hair boyishly short. The decade's nicknames, such as Jazz Age and Roaring Twenties, are clues to the mood of the times.

But the Jazz Age ended on a sour note. On October 29, 1929, the New York stock market crashed and investors lost billions of dollars. Almost overnight, the U.S. economy went into a downward spiral. Soon the economic slump spread worldwide, becoming known as the Great Depression. After the crash, banks and other businesses closed. Millions of Americans lost their jobs. Many families couldn't pay the rent and ended up homeless.

The economic slowdown affected everything from food to fashion, as average Americans struggled to make the most of every dollar. Many people made their own clothes, while others ordered clothing from the affordable Sears, Roebuck and Company catalog.

The Sears catalog of fall 1932 reflected the financial climate of the era. It stated, "These are not ordinary

Blouses and skirts were common fashion choices for women in the 1930s, as were fabrics with prints. Doris Carson, a musical actress of the time, shows off her look in 1933.

times." The copy went on, "We realize that economy [saving money] dictates that women must sew more this year . . . . Repairing, rather than replacing, will be the order in many families."

Changing Shapes

All the same, Americans craved new styles. Most clothing for women in the 1930s was relatively simple. Printed fabric was very popular, enlivening otherwise plain day dresses. Patterns included:

- **flowers**
- **plaids**
- **stripes**
- **tiny prints**

Clothing colors were darker than in the previous decade. Manufacturers of the 1930s also produced more inexpensive, man-made fabrics such as rayon.

Common fashions for women were blouses and skirts. Suits for women were also practical and popular. Skirt hemlines fell during the early thirties, with daytime fashions usually featuring calf-length skirts. Blouses often had high necklines and decorative soft, droopy bows. Later in the decade, blouses and gowns accentuated the shoulders. Sleeves often puffed out at the shoulders or sported fluttery ruffles. Suit jackets had chunky shoulder pads for extra emphasis.

FRUGAL FASHIONS

As Sears had predicted, many women altered their older clothes to fit new fashions during the Depression. They nipped in waists and added flounces and frills to hems. Homemade knitted clothes such as sweaters rose in popularity.

Sears provided an innovative money-saving solution by selling semi-made clothes. The buyer received partially sewn pieces, which she then finished sewing together. These pieces were less expensive than finished garments but less time-consuming than making clothes from scratch.

By the beginning of the 1930s, U.S. manufacturers produced more ready-to-wear clothing in standardized sizes than any other nation. The industry was a major part of U.S.

Actress Barbara Stanwyck wears a black dress with tulle sleeves in 1940. Puffy sleeves like these came into American fashion in the late 1930s. Stanwyck made eighty-five films in Hollywood before acting for television. She won three Emmy Awards and a Golden Globe.

business and formed the backbone of New York City's economy. In 1938 the influential fashion magazine *Vogue* described the flourishing ready-to-wear industry's impact on American fashion. "We are a clothes-crazy people," the article announced. "We boast that our shop-girls look as attractive as our social butterflies . . . we're even a little smug about being called, as we frequently are, the best-dressed women in the world." *Vogue* went on, "Actually, it isn't so much that we are the best-dressed—it is that *more* of us are well-dressed . . . collectively, en masse, our 40,000,000 adult females are better dressed, more fashion-conscious than any others on the face of the earth."

Vogue magazine is an influential fashion magazine in the United States. This *Vogue* cover from 1938 was illustrated by Georges Lepape.

One of the most revolutionary innovations in 1930s fashion seems pretty basic to modern dressers: the zipper. Zippers were not a brand-new invention. In fact, early versions of the zipper date back to the late 1800s. But their use in fashion was limited at first. They showed up mainly in men's accessories. For example, some galoshes and other men's boots zipped closed.

Zippers began appearing in women's clothing in the 1930s. Salespeople in some shops were trained in showing customers how to use the newfangled devices. Soon their convenience made them a hit. A 1930 advertisement exclaimed, "ZIP . . . open! ZIP . . . closed! That's the smart, smooth, modern way!"

Yet ready-to-wear clothing had drawbacks. The formfitting 1930s silhouette often made it difficult for a woman to find a garment that was correctly proportioned and sized for her particular body shape.

HOLLYWOOD GLAMOUR

In the midst of a gloomy economic period, moviegoing brought light into the lives of average Americans. It offered a welcome escape from the daily struggles that people faced during the Great Depression. A ticket to the movies cost about twenty-five cents in 1935. This low price made it possible for many Americans to scrounge up enough to see a picture once a week or so.

Meanwhile, Hollywood had entered an exciting new era. In 1927 the Warner Brothers movie studio had released *The Jazz Singer*. This film was billed as the first talkie—a film that had spoken dialogue. Previously, movies had musical sound tracks but no recorded dialogue. By the end of the 1920s, only a few silent films still trickled out of Hollywood. Talkies were here to stay.

As the new film genre caught on, new stars of the silver screen emerged. Actresses such as Marlene Dietrich, Greta Garbo, and Jean Harlow became fashion icons. Shops, pattern makers, and fashion lovers took note of on-screen trends. They adapted Hollywood inspiration into affordable garments. For instance, in 1935 a Sears catalog marketed a stylish party dress with the slogan, "The Long Sleeve—a New Hollywood Success." The dress was priced at an affordable $4.98.

Actress Marlene Dietrich was a glamorous fashion icon whom designers and American women imitated. Here, she wears a translucent white gown in 1936.

Ladies of Leisure

The 1930s saw a rise in sportswear for women. The active woman could choose outfits for activities such as:

- **tennis**
- **golf**
- **horseback riding**
- **skiing**

Some of these fashions had skirts. Those that had slacks usually featured wide legs.

Another leisure fashion of the 1930s was the "playsuit" for women. These outfits generally consisted of simple tops and flared, longish shorts. They were comfortable and lightweight, suitable for picnics and hikes.

Bathing suits in the thirties showed more skin than ever before. Low-cut backs allowed bathing beauties to get trendy, even suntans. The perfect tan was a necessity for the daring, backless evening gowns that were fashionable at the time. Jantzen was the main U.S. producer of swimwear. The company made good use of new man-made materials that were stretchy and flexible.

Yet another new leisure fashion was the dinner pajama. This loose, one- or two-piece garment was usually made of soft, flowing fabric such as silk. Most dinner pajamas sported a divided skirt—a pair of pants with wide, full legs. The pajama craze shifted formerly private, casual wear into the public realm. A 1931 newspaper article described the fad, saying, "There are pajamas in which to cook the ham . . . and for a dash to the corner grocery."

Other leisure wear was decidedly more practical. Women's overalls appeared in the Sears catalog in 1930 for the first time. The catalog exclaimed, "Everybody's wearing them!"

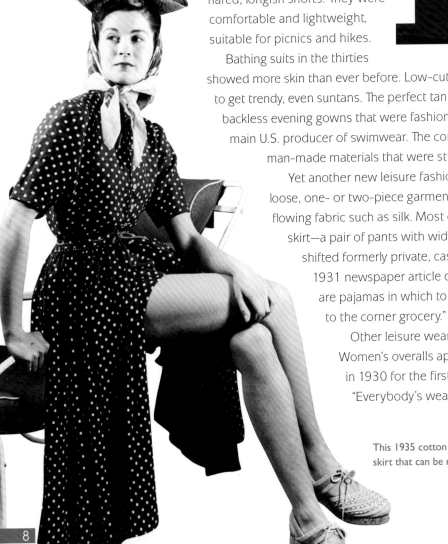

A woman plays tennis in activewear, which became increasingly popular in the 1930s.

This 1935 cotton playsuit features polka-dot fabric and a full skirt that can be removed to show shorts.

WOMEN AT WAR

Just as the end of the 1920s brought dark days, so did the close of the 1930s. World War II (1939–1945) erupted when Germany, under the Nazi leader Adolf Hitler, invaded Poland. The United States officially entered World War II in late 1941 on the side of Great Britain, France, and the other Allied nations. The Allies fought the Axis powers, which included Germany and Japan. Tens of thousands of Americans—nearly all of them men—left for war.

As the war dragged on, American women began taking on new duties and responsibilities outside the home. Thousands took jobs in factories, making goods for the armed forces as well as for the home front. The U.S. Labor Department assured women that they were ready for these tasks. "If you've

Rosie the Riveter posters portrayed working women during World War II. This version was created by the Westinghouse company in 1942.

used an electric mixer in your kitchen, you can learn to run a drill press," encouraged one pamphlet. (The pamphlet left out the fact that most women would be paid less than their male counterparts.)

A figure called Rosie the Riveter has become a symbol of women's contribution to the wartime economy. Rosie's image arose from a few different sources. In 1942 the Westinghouse company hired an artist to create a poster showing a young female factory worker. The woman wears overalls and has a red kerchief with white polka dots tied over her hair. Above her is the upbeat caption, "We Can Do It!"

A real woman had modeled for the poster's artist. However, the poster didn't identify her by name—and her name wasn't Rosie. But then a patriotic song from 1942 coined the name Rosie the Riveter. And the following year, popular artist Norman Rockwell created a cover for the magazine the *Saturday Evening Post* that showed a female factory worker. Rockwell titled his piece *Rosie the Riveter*. From then on, the name stuck and a character was born.

American women joined the armed forces in large numbers. About 350,000 American women joined special units including:

- **the Women's Army Corp** (WAC)
- **the Women Airforce Service Pilot** (WASPs)
- **the Women Accepted for Volunteer Emergency Services** (WAVES)

Enlisted women put on official uniforms. A 1943 WAVES recruiting pamphlet presented the wardrobe as a perk of the job. It urged, "Picture yourself in these smart Navy Uniforms."

"MAKE and MEND"

In 1942 the U.S. War Production Board introduced Regulation L-85. It rationed (limited) how much material—as well as what kinds of fabrics—could be used in making clothing. Wool, cotton, silk, and nylon were all restricted. They were needed to make uniforms, parachutes, and other goods for the war. Detailed guidelines dictated how much fabric was allowed in various garments. Full skirts requiring a lot of fabric disappeared, and fancy trimmings such as fur and lace were rare. Fewer printed fabrics were seen, since some dyes were limited too.

During the war, many women made clothes at home. *Vogue* and other magazines suggested ways to make every dollar count. Articles recommended tactics for covering old shoes with new fabric, reusing buttons, and trimming hats with material left over from other projects. Some sources even showed how to take apart men's suits and sew the pieces into feminine fashions. One 1944 pamphlet on

This 1940s pamphlet called *Make and Mend for Victory* gave suggestions on how to re-create existing clothes and make inexpensive accessories to brighten up an old wardrobe. Fabrics were limited during World War II. This booklet was filled with ideas to help make do with what Americans had available.

home sewing was titled *Make and Mend for Victory*.

The postwar years witnessed a big fashion milestone—or, actually, a tiny one. In the summer of 1946, two French men took swimwear to a new extreme: the bikini. Fashion historians disagree about exactly who came up with the idea first. Louis Réard, a French auto engineer, and clothing designer Jacques Heim both presented their versions of bikinis that year.

The two-piece bathing suit was not a brand-new idea. It had appeared in the 1930s and gained popularity in the 1940s, in part because of wartime rationing. Two-piece suits simply used less fabric. But earlier two-piece designs had one major difference: they covered the belly button. Revealing the navel in public was considered taboo.

The suit's makers embraced the taboo. Heim described his creation as the smallest swimsuit ever. Not to be outdone, Réard insisted that his was even smaller. Heim dubbed his version *atome*—French for "atom," the smallest unit of matter then known. Réard called his the bikini, and his label stuck. Réard got the name from a Pacific chain of islands called the Bikini Atoll—the site of nuclear bomb tests beginning in 1946. Réard apparently believed that his suit's impact would be similar to that of a bomb.

The skimpy French suits did shock many people. Several countries banned them. Nevertheless, some celebrities—including French actress Brigitte Bardot and American movie star Marilyn Monroe—embraced the daring style. It took longer for average women to adopt the look. By the late 1950s, a few bikinis were showing up on U.S. beaches—but many onlookers still disapproved.

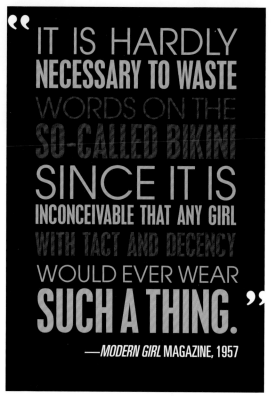

Bikinis were invented in France in 1946 and quickly became popular in the United States. This woman models a bikini on the beach in the 1950s.

"IT IS HARDLY NECESSARY TO WASTE WORDS ON THE SO-CALLED BIKINI SINCE IT IS INCONCEIVABLE THAT ANY GIRL WITH TACT AND DECENCY WOULD EVER WEAR SUCH A THING."

—*MODERN GIRL* MAGAZINE, 1957

BOBBY-SOXERS AND BLUE JEANS

The term *bobby-soxer* originated in the 1940s to describe female fans of crooner Frank Sinatra. These girls and young women often wore short white ankle socks called bobby socks. By the fifties, the term had become more general, describing a wider group of teenage girls.

In addition to the signature socks, bobby-soxers often wore poodle skirts. These full skirts fell below the knee and came in a range of colors, though pink was the classic choice. Giving the garment its name, a fuzzy image of a poodle was sewn onto the skirt with yarn. Young women often paired their poodle skirts with white button-up shirts. Another common choice with a skirt was a fitted cardigan sweater. Lace trim, beaded patterns, or decorative buttons added youthful flair.

Another classic 1950s look was the twin set—a crewneck pullover sweater paired with a fitted cardigan in the same color. Worn with a simple strand of pearls, the look was stylishly simple. In fact, the phrase "twin set and pearls" came to represent casual fifties chic.

In the 1940s, some teens and women started to wear blue jeans for casual wear rather than for factory work.

Many teenage girls and young women of the 1950s wore poodle skirts. The full, swinging skirts featured yarn poodles.

But not everybody wore twin sets. In fact, more teenage girls and young women started wearing blue jeans. Young people no longer saw jeans as work clothes only. They wanted to wear them to school, to the movies, and to hang out with friends. However, most schools didn't allow students to attend classes in jeans. Some theaters and restaurants refused to serve people wearing jeans, which were viewed as too casual.

Singer-actress Dinah Shore wears a little black dress in the 1950s. Her version of the sleeveless, belted, black dress included petticoats for extra volume in the skirt.

FABULOUS FIFTIES

Even as casual looks flourished, glamour was still very much in style in the fifties. One chic look was the basic black sheath dress. The sheath was close-fitting and sleek. It was usually sleeveless, with a hemline near the knee, and most of the time, the waist was belted or cinched. Although sheaths came in many colors, black was the classic choice. In 1952 *Vogue* declared that "the little black dress, deceptively simple, is the core of every collection."

Elizabeth Taylor, Grace Kelly, Audrey Hepburn, and Marilyn Monroe were among the decade's big film stars. Their outfits—on-screen and off—especially influenced evening gowns. Sleeveless and strapless looks were common. While most gowns were floor-length, some had hemlines at mid-calf. Bows were a popular decoration, whether they were big and showy or small and sweet. Colors included

- **soft pastels**
- **bold reds**
- **sophisticated blacks and whites**

For American girls, the ultimate chance to indulge in glamour was the prom. The springtime dance was a highlight of the year for many high school students.

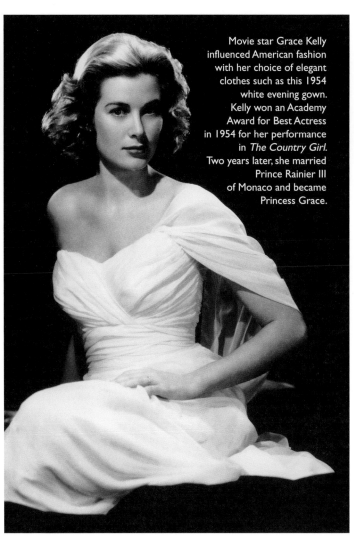

Movie star Grace Kelly influenced American fashion with her choice of elegant clothes such as this 1954 white evening gown. Kelly won an Academy Award for Best Actress in 1954 for her performance in *The Country Girl*. Two years later, she married Prince Rainier III of Monaco and became Princess Grace.

The Lobster Dress, created in 1937 by Elsa Schiaparelli, can now be seen at the Philadelphia Museum of Art in Pennsylvania. Schiaparelli was known for creating out-of-the-ordinary clothes.

Chapter Two

WOMEN'S HAUTE COUTURE

Haute couture is a French phrase that means "high dressmaking" or "high sewing." The term has come to refer to the whole world of creating high-quality, high-fashion clothing. Haute couture designers, also called couturiers, often produce one-of-a-kind garments. Some of these pieces are more like works of art than clothes. Couturiers also create custom-made clothes for specific clients. A variety of influences, movements, and trends affected these designers.

HEIGHTENED REALITY

In the 1930s, an artistic movement called surrealism was taking the art world by storm. Surrealists such as Spanish artist Salvador Dalí depicted surprising and sometimes absurd combinations of subjects and images. For instance, one of Dalí's most famous works was a telephone with a lobster for a receiver.

Surrealism heavily influenced the Italian clothing designer Elsa Schiaparelli. Schiaparelli's clothes were daring and sometimes strange. One of her famous pieces was the 1937 Lobster Dress. It was a white, floor-length dress of silk, with a wide reddish band under the bust. What made it really unusual was the enormous lobster on the skirt—painted by Dalí himself.

WORDS
OF WISDOM

The clothing of haute couture designer Elsa Schiaparelli was frequently fantastic. But she also had a practical side. In 1936 she offered women down-to-earth fashion advice. She confided, "I wear suits nearly all of the time. I like them; they are practical in every way, and my advice to a business girl who wishes to dress smartly at all times and whose income is very limited is this: buy a good suit and live in it."

French designer Coco Chanel was known for her suit designs. This suit from 1959 has the Chanel look. It features clean lines with no jacket lapels.

Schiaparelli used brightly colored zippers on some of her garments, making a dramatic visual statement. She was fond of buttons in whimsical shapes, including

- **horses**
- **swans**
- **acrobats**

Schiaparelli even had a signature color: shocking pink, better known in modern times as hot pink.

THE CHANEL SUIT

French designer Gabrielle Chanel—who was known by her nickname Coco—created high-fashion women's suits. The Chanel suit was notable for its clean lines. Jackets were slightly boxy, and many had simple, round collars and no lapels. Skirts were slim and straight. Variations of Chanel's look hit the streets across Europe and the United States. While not every woman could afford a real Chanel suit, a chic and streamlined suit soon became an essential piece in the fashionable woman's wardrobe.

Coco Chanel had a way of being practical and fashion forward at the same time. For instance, she began using cotton in evening wear. Previously, most people considered cotton best suited to day dresses and casual blouses. But Chanel helped make cotton fashionable after dark. The material was versatile and affordable, making it a good choice during the cost-cutting 1930s.

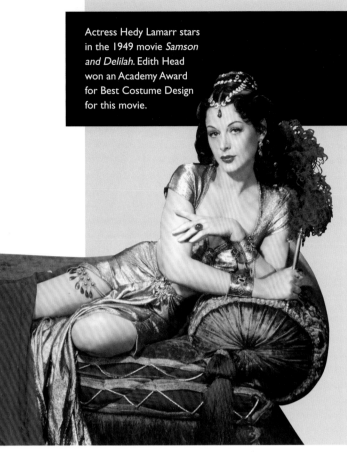

THE QUEEN OF COSTUME

For more than half a century, Edith Head was the indisputable queen of film fashion. Her long costuming career began in the late 1920s, and it didn't end until her death in 1981. During that time, she worked on more than four hundred movies and dressed major stars including Bette Davis, Ginger Rogers, Grace Kelly, Audrey Hepburn, and Elizabeth Taylor. She was also nominated for more than thirty Academy Awards, receiving nominations every single year between 1948 and 1966. She won the Oscar eight times—more than any other woman in cinema history.

SOLDIERING ON

For decades, France had been the center of international fashion. Parisian runways dictated what was hot—and what was not—around the world. But the cost of importing custom-made gowns from Europe was far too high for most Americans during the Depression. U.S. department stores and other buyers drastically reduced orders from foreign fashion houses. American shoppers began turning more attention toward designers working closer to home and toward affordable but chic ready-to-wear garments. Successful American designers of the 1930s included Clare Potter and Elizabeth Hawes.

The designers who did survive the lean years of the Depression faced new challenges with the outbreak of World War II. Materials and labor were both in increasingly short supply. It also seemed that worrying about the cut of a fashionable gown while thousands of people died on battlefields was frivolous and inappropriate—even immoral.

Nevertheless, nations that had boasted strong fashion industries, such as France and Britain, wanted to maintain that source of income even in wartime. *Vogue* magazine put on a brave face about the future of fashion during the conflict. "As long as there is desire for change and love of self-expression, a sense of fitness and sense of fantasy—there will be fashion."

European couturiers did continue to produce collections, but they had to work within limits. Rationing in Britain was especially strict, and the resulting clothes were known as utility wear. An article describing rationed fashions said, "Designs are, of course, within the new austerity specification: only so many buttons, this much cuff and that much skirt."

Nevertheless, with German troops occupying Paris and London facing nightly bombing during some periods of the conflict, the war took its toll on European fashion. As early as the autumn of 1940, the tide had begun to turn in favor of U.S. designers. *Ladies' Home Journal* exclaimed, "America claims its own! This year, as never before, all eyes turn to New York for fashion guidance." Vera Maxwell and Muriel King were among the home-front designers who gained in prominence.

The New Look

Christian Dior's New Look is modeled in 1947. Dior used many yards of fancy fabric to create this small-waisted and full-skirted fashion.

After the war ended, many Americans wanted to go back to enjoying life. Fashion was one way to do this. Fortunately for the stylish set, the war's end meant that rationing limits were lifted in Europe and the United States. A Sears catalog of the time expressed relief at the end of wartime shortages. Advertising three stylish dresses, the copy gushed, "Skirts are longer. . . . Fabrics are used lavishly. Trimmings are brilliant."

French designer Christian Dior took advantage of these new freedoms. In 1947 he released a collection that took the fashion world by storm. It came to be known simply as the New Look. Dior's collection left behind the war's blunt, straight-edged look. His designs returned to the feminine silhouette that had begun to emerge in the 1930s—and took it further with:

- **gentle, sloping shoulders**
- **tailored jackets** nipped in tightly to accentuate tiny waists
- **huge, full skirts** billowing from the hips
- **hemlines below the mid-calf**

Dior described his approach and his inspiration. "I designed clothes for flower-like women, with rounded shoulders, full, feminine busts, and hand-span waists above enormous, spreading skirts."

The look proved to be a bit *too* new for some observers. They criticized Dior's lavish collection, arguing that such showy clothes were inappropriate in the wake of the war's tragedies. In particular, the great expanses of fabric in Dior designs raised eyebrows. Some women resented the return to the restrictions of long skirts. One Texan housewife founded the Little Below the Knee Club. Other women protested at stores that sold Dior's looks, holding signs that read, "Mr. Dior, We abhor Dresses To the floor."

> **MANY PEOPLE DISMISS HAUTE COUTURE AS** BEING SOMETHING THAT IS ONLY FOR THOSE WHO ARE VERY WEALTHY.... SIMPLICITY, GOOD TASTE, AND GROOMING ARE THE **THREE FUNDAMENTALS OF GOOD DRESSING** AND THESE DO NOT COST MONEY.
>
> —CHRISTIAN DIOR IN THE INTRODUCTION TO HIS *LITTLE DICTIONARY OF FASHION,* 1954

Yet out of the uproar, Dior quickly emerged as one of the world's top high-fashion designers. *Vogue* praised Dior's collection as the dawn of a new age in fashion. "There are moments when fashion changes fundamentally. . . . This is one of those moments."

FROM ALPHABET SOUP TO
THE FLYING TRAPEZE

By the mid-1950s, Dior's new looks included several alphabet-inspired designs. The A-line featured dresses and jackets that were narrow at the shoulders and then widened diagonally into swingy hemlines. The resulting shape resembled the letter *A.* The Y-line was the reverse: it had slim skirts and slightly wide, exaggerated necklines and shoulders. And the H-line was a middle ground, with the narrow waistlines Dior loved in between well-balanced shoulders and skirts.

This 1954 H-line ensemble by Christian Dior features a slender black wool double-breasted jacket with five horizontal rows of buttons and a straight skirt. The H-line dropped the jacket hemline from the waist to the hips.

Christian Dior died suddenly in 1957. Young French designer Yves Saint Laurent, who had worked for Dior, took over the influential fashion house. He was only twenty-one years old.

The youthful Saint Laurent took the Dior label in a fresh, bold direction. He presented his first collection as the head of the fashion house in the spring of 1958. The haute couture world was somewhat skeptical about the show. As *Time* magazine reported, "In the crystal-chandeliered salon, the press was dead silent as the first model swirled in, wearing a sprig of Dior's favorite flower, lily of the valley, on her suit."

But doubt quickly turned to delight. "As the third model sashayed out, sudden applause . . . crashed through the cream-and-gilt rooms. . . . Cries of 'bravo, bravo!' broke out at the finale."

Saint Laurent's Trapeze line was the reason for the applause. Its silhouette was slightly relaxed and softly swinging. Trapeze jackets and dresses were narrow at the shoulders, widening gradually as they fell. Skirts were fitted rather loosely at the waist and were gently flared but not overly full.

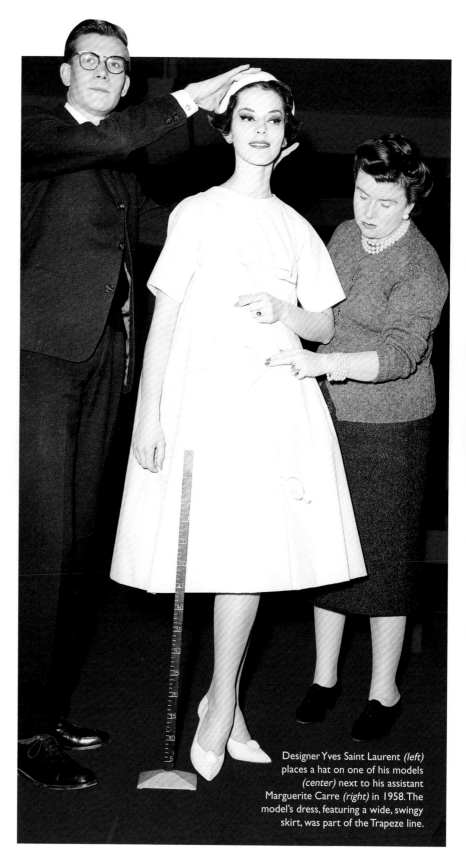

Designer Yves Saint Laurent *(left)* places a hat on one of his models *(center)* next to his assistant Marguerite Carre *(right)* in 1958. The model's dress, featuring a wide, swingy skirt, was part of the Trapeze line.

ALTA MODA

European fashion trends had influenced American style for many years. For example, major Italian figures of earlier years had included surrealist designer Elsa Schiaparelli, shoe and handbag designer Guccio Gucci, and shoe designer to the stars Salvatore Ferragamo. But beginning in the early 1950s, many newer Italian designers were finding greater success and a wider audience. A 1953 article reported, "Couture in Rome and Florence and Milan has been a volcano in constant eruption of ideas, some wonderful, some not, all of them executed with . . . inventiveness and superb working materials." Recognized names of Italian *alta moda* (high fashion) included Roberto Capucci, Emilio Pucci, Oleg Cassini, Valentino Garavani (usually known only as Valentino), and married designers—and competitors—Alberto Fabiani and Simonetta Visconti. Italian fashion was elegant, inventive, modern, and chic. Meanwhile, popular Italian film stars such as Gina Lollobrigida and Sophia Loren brought Italian glamour to American moviegoers. By the end of the decade, Italy had firmly established itself as one of the world's most stylish nations.

Italian actress Gina Lollobrigida *(left)* shows off the gown Italian designer Emilio Schuberth *(right)* created for her to wear to a film festival in 1954. After Lollobrigida's acting career died down, she embarked on a successful career in photojournalism.

Wedding Wear

During the 1930s through the 1950s, many women who could afford it donned custom-made, high-fashion wedding dresses. At the beginning of the 1930s, some bridal gowns had mid-length hemlines. But many others were full-length. High necklines and long rows of dainty, cloth-covered buttons were common.

The Duchess of Windsor, Wallis Simpson *(left)*, stands next to the Duke of Windsor on their wedding day in France. Simpson was an American who married the British duke in 1937. She wore a Mainbocher wedding dress.

One notable wedding gown of the thirties belonged to Wallis Simpson, the Duchess of Windsor. Simpson was an American woman who married Britain's Duke of Windsor. (The duke had been, very briefly, Britain's king but gave up the throne to marry Simpson. At the time, marrying a divorced woman was unacceptable for a British king.) Simpson was renowned for her sense of fashion. In 1937 she chose the American couturier Mainbocher to design her wedding dress:

- **a slim, floor-length gown**
- **a matching jacket** with a fitted waist
- **a ruffled bib over the bust**

The ensemble was a pale blue that came to be called Wallis blue.

During World War II, U.S. rationing did not apply to bridal wear. The government thought that limiting such special garments would damage morale on the home front. Nevertheless, many wartime brides wore suits or simple dresses instead of elaborate gowns.

In the late 1940s and the 1950s, wedding gowns became flouncy and romantic. Yards of pleated fabric were common, and lace was the most common trim. Some gowns were calf-length rather than floor-length. They featured the cinched waists and full skirts of the New Look.

Chapter Three

MEN'S CLOTHING

Men's fashions of the 1930s were more fitted than they had been in the 1920s. For example, jackets narrowed slightly through the waist. The overall silhouette was still fairly boxy, however. Shoulders were wide, to emphasize an athletic appearance. In the middle of the decade, trousers were slightly tapered. Most suits were double-breasted, with two rows of buttons on the jacket. The three-piece suit remained the standard style. Common colors included gray, black, brown, and tan, and patterns included plaids and pinstripes.

For dressy events, many men wore black tuxedos. They often had satin lapels and were worn with a white shirt and sometimes a white vest. Especially dressy tuxedos had tailcoats, which were short in front and long in back.

As the Depression held the United States in its grip, many men couldn't afford new suits—much less tuxedos. However, for a relatively small amount of money, men could buy new shirts and ties, helping to give their old suits a fresh look.

The Sporting Life

Sportswear and leisure wear were important aspects of men's fashion during this era. Sears sold wide-legged sport trousers in light, comfortable fabrics

This man wears a double-breasted suit in 1939. A double-breasted suit jacket has two columns of buttons and wide, overlapping lapels.

Jimmy McDaniel hits a shot during a tennis game in New York in 1940. He wears a T-shirt tucked tightly into his white, pleated pants, as was the style. McDaniel won many matches in tennis, which was a segregated sport at this time.

such as linen and white flannel. The catalog exclaimed, "For the Good Old Summertime: Yes! They're Cool!"

Sweaters were very popular among stylish, sporty men. Some were thick and rugged. Others were finer, and many sported patterns, either through differently colored yarn or through textures such as cable knits. Cardigans and V-necks were common styles.

Off the battlefield, men in the mid-1940s loved casual trousers with pleats and high waists. Men generally wore these pants with

- **sweaters**
- **button-down shirts**
- **T-shirts**
- **or some combination of the above**

Men tucked the tops snugly into the waistband.

Meanwhile, sunbathing shirtless became common among men for the first time. Previously, men had worn full-length bathing suits. In the 1930s and the 1940s, swimming trunks hit the beach. Trunks were basically just long shorts. Men wore these swimsuits well above the waist to cover the navel for proper modesty.

MEN IN UNIFORM

When World War II erupted, everyday wear suddenly became a uniform for millions of American men. Military uniforms were not meant as style statements. They were designed to be functional. Nevertheless, they played a big role in defining the look of the era. In general, officers had the dressiest uniforms. They usually wore closely fitted jackets paired with perfectly pressed trousers. Officers' jackets sported medals, badges, and ribbons representing their ranks and achievements.

Lower-ranking enlisted men wore more basic uniforms. Many U.S. Army soldiers—especially those serving in hot climates—sported fatigues. These uniforms included loose-fitting pants and long-sleeved button-down shirts. They were made of khaki, a strong cotton fabric in a sandy, tan color.

In U.S. port cities such as New York and San Francisco, off-duty sailors were a common sight during the war. They were easily identified by their uniform:

- **loose-fitting white shirt**
- **white pants**
- **long black neckerchief**
- **soft white cap**

This U.S. sailor poses in his sailor uniform for a portrait with his wife and child in 1945.

TIGHTENING BELTS

Rationing affected men's clothes during the war. The three-piece suit—trousers, vest, and jacket—had once been the norm. But the vest fell out of favor, as tailors decided that limited supplies of fabric could be put to better use. Some men wore vests after the war, especially for dressy occasions. But they were never again a standard part of the man's suit.

Similarly, the single-breasted suit, with one row of buttons down the front of the jacket, became more common during the war. Its slimmer, sleeker cut required less material than the boxy, broad-shouldered double-breasted suit of earlier years. Pleats and cuffs were other fabric-consuming details that disappeared from most trousers during the war.

ZOOT SUIT STYLE

One unique men's fashion of the 1940s was the zoot suit. This exaggerated, oversized suit featured trousers with a high waist and wide legs that tapered to narrower cuffs. The jacket was long and roomy and had wide shoulders.

This distinctive style was especially popular among minority groups in the United States. In particular, many African Americans and Mexican Americans sported zoot suits. These groups faced discrimination and hostility from some of their fellow Americans. Zoot suits used a lot of fabric, going against World War II rationing. Wearing these suits during wartime represented rebellion.

Many zoot suiters saw their clothes as a protest against a society that discriminated against them. However, the garb took on a different meaning outside the minority community. Many people came to associate zoot suits with troublemaking and crime.

These fashionable teens wear zoot suits in 1943. The word *zoot* probably came about because it rhymes with the word *suit*.

Aloha!

When World War II ended, American soldiers brought some battlefield fashions back to U.S. shores. Chinos—sometimes called khakis because of their color—were among these imports. During the war, U.S. soldiers had worn these comfortable, durable trousers as part of their uniform. Back home, they became popular among college students. And thanks to a 1944 law known as the G.I. Bill, thousands of men were attending college. The bill offered university educations to veterans of the war.

Another casual postwar fashion was the short-sleeved, front-buttoned Hawaiian shirt.

President Harry Truman sports a popular style—the Hawaiian shirt—while in Florida in 1948. Truman was the thirty-third president of the United States and took office in 1945 after President Franklin Roosevelt's death.

(During the war, many U.S. servicemen were stationed on Pacific islands, including Hawaii.) Sometimes known as aloha shirts, Hawaiian shirts sported bright, colorful prints with

- **flowers**
- **leaves**
- **tropical patterns**

The vivid shirts grew in popularity in the 1950s, when Hawaii was a fashionable vacation spot. Sears marketed Hawaiian-inspired sports shirts and sold them for $1.87 apiece.

On the other end of the fashion spectrum, the suit remained the classic choice for the well-dressed man. Tailors were once again free to use as much material as they liked. Double-breasted jackets returned, along with wider lapels and broader shoulders. Pleats and cuffs returned to many suits.

Yet some men continued wearing slimmer single-breasted suits. For example, the gray flannel suit was a conservative, basic style common among men with office jobs. The look was so widespread that a popular movie made reference to it. *The Man in the Gray Flannel Suit*, starring Gregory Peck, was a 1956 film based on a novel of the same name.

For casual wear, many American men donned sport coats. Similar to suit jackets, sport coats came in a wider variety of colors, materials, and patterns. Daring dressers—usually teenagers and young men—wore sport coats in bright colors or in patterns such as wide stripes. Some men liked wearing a sport coat over a sweater, which itself was usually worn over a button-down shirt and a tie. Many sweaters sported basic designs such as stripes or argyles (a diamond pattern on a solid background).

This man wears a smoking jacket in 1950 while relaxing at home. A smoking jacket is usually made of velvet or silk and closes with a tie belt.

The smoking jacket was for fashionable lounging. Men wore these belted jackets while smoking after-dinner cigars, pipes, or cigarettes. A smoking jacket is looser and more comfortable than a suit coat or sport coat. It's still on the dressy side, however, and is usually made of velvet or silk. Suave stars such as Dean Martin, Frank Sinatra, Fred Astaire, and Cary Grant modeled the style.

EYE ON YOUTH

Before the 1950s, children and teenagers typically wore smaller versions of adult outfits. The 1950s marked the first time that a variety of clothing was designed specifically for younger dressers.

> " MY HUSBAND CAN BE WELL DRESSED FOR ALMOST ANY OCCASION WITH ONLY TWO OR THREE SUITS IN HIS WARDROBE, BUT WITH ME IT'S DIFFERENT. MAYBE I CAN TRANSFORM AN OFFICE DRESS WITH THE ADDITION OF A ROSE OR A JEWEL, BUT YOU CAN DO JUST SO MUCH OF THIS AND GET BY. A DRESS THAT GOES WELL AT A COCKTAIL PARTY MIGHT FIT IN AT A WEDDING, BUT THE CHANCES ARE IT WON'T. "
>
> —*TIME* MAGAZINE QUOTING A YOUNG WOMAN, 1953

In the 1953 movie *The Wild One*, Marlon Brando *(center)* and his gang wear dark, rolled-up jeans; black leather jackets; and black leather boots. Many young men copied this rebellious style.

Hollywood was a big part of the youth-oriented fashion trend. Hit films of the time included 1953's *The Wild One*, starring Marlon Brando, and 1955's *Rebel Without a Cause*, starring James Dean. These movies portrayed angry young men who didn't want to follow society's rules. Young American men began to model their wardrobes after Brando's *Wild One* character. They donned dark blue jeans rolled up at the cuffs, plain white T-shirts, and heavy black leather boots. Black leather jackets completed the rebellious look.

Jeans were also part of the beatnik wardrobe. A group of writers and artists called the Beats challenged social norms through their work. Important Beat books include Jack Kerouac's *On the Road* and Allen Ginsberg's *Howl and Other Poems*. The term *beatnik*, coined by a San Francisco newspaper writer in 1958, was meant as an insult. The media picture that emerged—beatniks dressed in black, brooding in coffeehouses, and writing bad poetry—was a caricature. Nevertheless, some young Americans did model their style on a beatnik image.

PROM KING

Just as high school girls had special dresses for the prom, boys also donned dressy but youthful evening wear. Some wore tuxedos, while others preferred sport coats, usually in pale, springy colors. A fresh flower on the lapel added the final festive touch.

These prom fashions even inspired a song. In 1957 Marty Robbins sang "A White Sport Coat (and a Pink Carnation)." The tune describes a teenage boy who has gotten all dressed up for the big dance. Unfortunately for him, his date decides to go with someone else.

A white jacket with a colored flower in the breast pocket was a typical prom look for young men in the 1950s.

Other young Americans took style cues from a new and exciting music scene—rockabilly, a mix of rock and country music. One of its major stars was singer Elvis Presley. Rockabilly lovers wore blue jeans, button-down shirts in stripes and plaids and bright colors as well as a lot of black and white.

The flip side of blue jeans and motorcycle jackets was the preppy look. The name comes from preparatory schools, or prep schools, which prepare students to attend prestigious universities. Preppy dressers wore conservative clothes such as sweater vests and sport coats. They often chose shirts and sweaters in pastel colors. Some also wore varsity sweaters and jackets sporting letters awarded to high school and college athletes.

The preppy look was the opposite of the rebellious look of the 1950s. Some preppies wore varsity letter sweaters like this one.

The head cutter at Savile Row, W. Smith *(left)*, takes measurements on a customer's suit in the fitting room in 1938.

MEN'S HAUTE COUTURE

During the 1930s through the 1950s, haute couture for men was limited. High-fashion menswear focused mainly on custom-made suits. For decades Savile Row—a street in central London—had been a major international center of men's tailor-made, high-end suits. Savile Row tailors used only the finest materials and took the most painstaking measurements to ensure the very best fit.

Some forward-thinking designers did create high-fashion menswear during these decades. René Lacoste and André Gillier formed Lacoste in 1933. The company's specialty was the tennis shirt, or polo shirt. These short-sleeved shirts had collars and buttons at the neck. The brand's trademark was a small crocodile logo on the chest. Lacoste shirts became popular with the preppy crowd of the 1950s and beyond.

In 1957 French designer Pierre Cardin opened a shop in Paris specifically for men's

SPEAK FOR YOURSELF!

A traditional term for a custom-made Savile Row suit is *bespoke*. The term comes from the verb *bespeak*, which means "to order something in advance." Similarly, a Savile Row tailor would say that a particular garment was "spoken for" by a specific customer.

clothing. His pieces included printed shirts and brightly colored neckties. Cardin also introduced a new, streamlined style of single-breasted suit. It had a high, round collar and no lapels. The look was sleek and modern.

Tennis players Bill Talbert *(left)* and Tony Trabert *(right)* wear Lacoste shirts, with the trademark crocodile, in the 1950s. A successful tennis star, Talbert mentored Trabert.

Actress Noel Francis wears her hair in a finger wave style in the 1930s. Noel Francis starred in movies such as *Blonde Crazy* (1931), *Smart Money* (1931), and *Stone of Silver Creek* (1935).

Chapter Four

HAIRSTYLES AND ACCESSORIES

Women's hairstyles of the 1930s were long and soft. Waves were the single must-have feature. Finger waves were a classic 1930s look. They were set at an angle and lay close to the scalp. To create finger waves, a stylish woman just needed a comb, fingers, wet hair—and patience. She used her fingers to guide the angle and width of the waves.

Other looks required rollers. Women wrapped and pinned sections of hair around cylindrical rollers of various sizes. Many women placed their hair in rollers before going to bed and slept on them overnight. The next morning, they took out the rollers and styled the curls. That night they'd start the routine all over again.

Rollers did the job, but they were a bit of a pain—especially since the curls didn't last. In the late 1800s, some European hairdressers had begun developing ways to create longer-lasting waves. Beginning in about 1930, a combination of chemicals and heat allowed for "permanent waves," or perms. While perms lasted a lot longer than finger curls and rollers, they weren't really permanent. Women returned to their beauty parlors every three months for fresh perms.

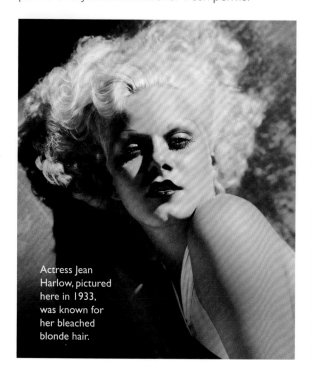

Actress Jean Harlow, pictured here in 1933, was known for her bleached blonde hair.

BLONDE BOMBSHELLS

The 1930s brought a fad for blonde hair. A number of popular actresses of the thirties had blonde hair. But it wasn't always their natural color. Jean Harlow, for example, bleached her hair to such a light blonde that it was almost white. Her famously pale locks earned her nicknames including the Blonde Bombshell and the Platinum Blonde. Inspired by Harlow's style, women across the United States went to their hairdressers asking for the same color. But the perfect shade came with a cost. Bleaching relied on the chemicals ammonia and peroxide—hence the term *peroxide blonde*. When used too often—or incorrectly—these harsh chemicals could lead to headaches, burned scalps, and hair loss.

Stylish Snoods and Chic Chignons

In the 1930s, pin curls rose in popularity. To create this look, women carefully twisted their hair into dozens of small curls, holding them in place with bobby pins. Like rollers, the pins usually stayed in overnight. The next day, they came out, leaving tightly waved hair. For dressy evening events, some women sported elaborate arrangements of curls piled on top of the head.

During World War II, many women wore their hair pinned back from the face. Women who took jobs in factories kept their hair shorter or took other measures to prevent accidents when working with machinery. One trend of the 1930s and the 1940s was the snood. This hairnet or fabric bag gathered up the hair and held it at the back of the head. The stylish look was also practical. Some working women during the war favored snoods for safety reasons.

In the late 1940s and the early 1950s, the chignon, a simple bun, was the height of sophistication. The bun could be placed anywhere from the crown of the head to the nape of the neck. The chignon was easy yet elegant. Artificial chignons in a range of colors appeared in shops and salons. Women whose hair wasn't long enough for the hairstyle could still stay chic by wearing these wiglike accessories.

This college student wears a snood in 1939. A snood, made of fabric or yarn, pulls hair away from the face.

TV LAND

Lucille Ball wore a poodle cut in 1955.

Television was making a mark on style in the 1950s. The number of families with TV sets skyrocketed during this decade. Like movies, television shows influenced fashion and reflected the mood of the times. But TV was different from film in two major ways. First, people didn't have to leave their homes to view TV shows. The images came right into the American family room. Second, movies often portrayed scenes of luxury and grandeur. Many television shows of the era, however, tended to be about home life. Shows such as *The Donna Reed Show* and *Father Knows Best* showed fairly average families going about their days and nights.

Some people got ideas for hairstyles from these shows. For example, Lucille Ball—star of the hit comedy *I Love Lucy*—sported a poodle cut. Donna Reed, on the other hand, wore a longer, softly waved style. People also paid close attention to the clothes they saw on TV. From Donna Reed's slim suits to Lucille Ball's full-skirted day dresses, American women took fashion cues from small-screen stars.

PONIES AND POODLES
AND PAGEBOYS, OH MY!

In the 1950s, ponytails were a popular choice for teenage girls and young women, especially bobby-soxers. Usually they wore the ponytail high on the head and waved the hair for extra bounce.

Another 1950s do was the poodle haircut. This look features short, tight curls, similar to a poodle's hair. A version of the pageboy hairstyle was also popular in the 1950s. Pageboy cuts ended above the shoulder, and the ends curled under. The cut sometimes included short bangs.

WHAT'S THE BUZZ?

Male hairstyles in the 1930s were simple and sophisticated. Men kept their hair short and neat. Along with a haircut, barbers also gave customers a close shave. Movie star Clark Gable sported a handsome mustache in many of his films, and mustaches became very stylish.

During World War II, the military required servicemen to wear their hair very short. The military cut is often called a buzz cut, since a buzzing electric razor trims the hair close to the scalp.

After the war, very short cuts remained common among some men—especially military veterans. A related men's hairstyle was the flattop, which became popular in the 1950s. Like a buzz cut or a crew cut, the flattop is very short overall, with the hair on the top of the head longer than on the sides. This longer hair then bristles upward into a flat surface.

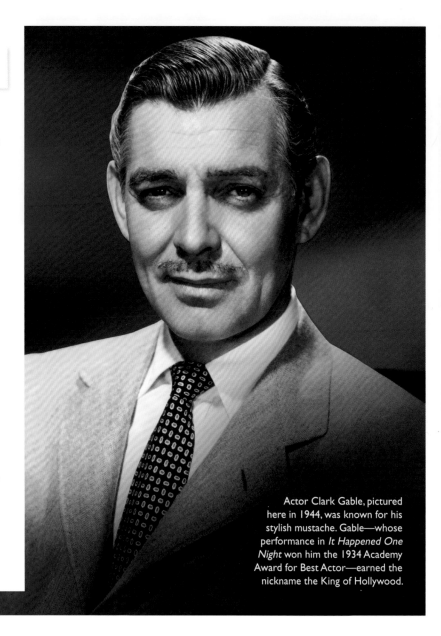

Actor Clark Gable, pictured here in 1944, was known for his stylish mustache. Gable—whose performance in *It Happened One Night* won him the 1934 Academy Award for Best Actor—earned the nickname the King of Hollywood.

James Dean wears his hair in a pompadour style while promoting his 1955 movie *Rebel Without a Cause*. In this film—Dean's best-known work—he plays a troubled teen in Los Angeles.

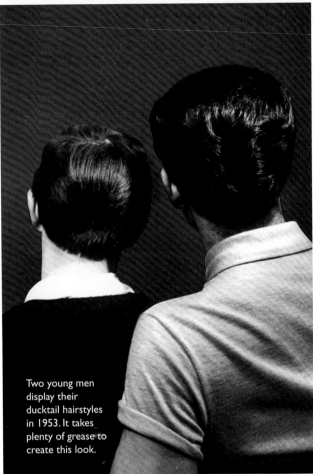

Two young men display their ducktail hairstyles in 1953. It takes plenty of grease to create this look.

POMPADOURS AND CIRCUMSTANCE

Movie star James Dean sported a pompadour in the 1950s. This hairstyle swept the hair up and back from the forehead, without a part. Men used hair products such as pomade to create and hold the style.

Some young men preferred the ducktail, slicking their hair back with plenty of pomade. At the back of the neck, the hair tapered down into a point. The shape resembled a duck's tail. Rock-and-roll megastar Elvis Presley favored the ducktail style. Elvis was hugely popular among young people. But he was also controversial—especially among parents—for his defiant image and his sexy dance moves.

"WHAT YOU WEAR WITH WHAT"

Hollywood's influence on fashion was especially clear when it came to accessories. Not every American woman could afford a couture ball gown or a full-length fur coat. But little items were easier to manage, even on a small budget, and could make even an old dress seem new again. *Vogue* magazine stressed the importance of finding the perfect items to complement an outfit. "It's not what you wear, but What you Wear with What."

During the thirties through the fifties, women wore hats for all occasions and in many styles. French berets were a hit in the 1930s. These soft, flat hats were made of wool or felt and were worn at a jaunty angle. They were ideal for casual outings and for sports such as golf.

In the late 1940s and the 1950s, cartwheel hats were popular. Very flat, with a wide, circular brim and a low crown, the cartwheel hat was made of straw, felt, or other materials. Decorations on these hats included feathers or artificial flowers.

Hats with black or white veils were another highly fashionable look. Veils ranged from basic mesh to patterned lace. Some hung loosely in front of the face, while others fit quite tightly. The latter was a stylish look, but not always a convenient one when it came time for eating or drinking.

Keeping a hat on was not easy. Some hats perched on the head. Others had very wide brims. A single gust of wind was enough to carry either style away. To keep hats secure—and at the perfect angle—women used long hatpins to attach their hats to their hair. Usually a decorative hatpin head showed on the outside of the hat.

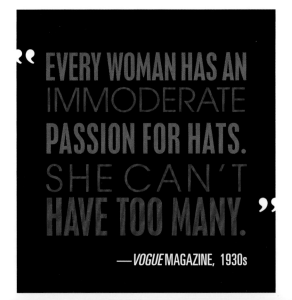

"EVERY WOMAN HAS AN IMMODERATE PASSION FOR HATS. SHE CAN'T HAVE TOO MANY."

—*VOGUE* MAGAZINE, 1930s

STAYING WARM AND LOOKING COOL

When temperatures dropped, women in the 1930s through the 1950s could choose from a variety of fashions to keep them warm. Coats very often had fur trim. Fur was also a popular

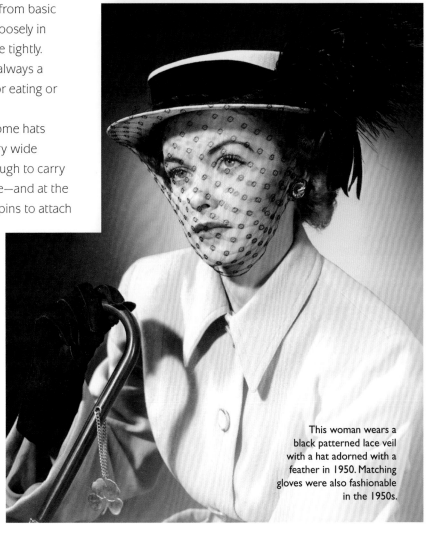

This woman wears a black patterned lace veil with a hat adorned with a feather in 1950. Matching gloves were also fashionable in the 1950s.

material for stoles and shoulder wraps, which became common in the 1950s.

One classic 1950s coat was the bolero. This short jacket ends above the waist and is open at the front. Paired with a narrow-waisted New Look dress, it made a striking ensemble.

Stylish ladies of the era wore gloves when they went out. Daytime gloves were short and made of cotton. Many women paired matching gloves and hats, sometimes in the same pattern

Actress Myrna Loy wears a coat with fur trim in 1934. Fur was popular for outerwear until the animal rights movement began in the 1970s.

This woman models a dress with a matching bolero jacket in 1953. A bolero is like a shrug but more formal.

or with the same lacy trim. Evening gloves were long and made of silk or satin, sometimes dyed to match the hue of a woman's gown. Fancy evening gloves featured decorations such as gems.

Scarves were also popular accessories. One 1933 Sears catalog exclaimed, "A colorful scarf is the spice of the outfit!" For women riding in convertibles, head scarves were a must. During World War II, most automobile plants had shifted to making goods for the war. But after the war's end, car manufacturing began again—and Americans were eager to buy. The Sunday drive became a family tradition. To prevent mussing their carefully styled hair on these rides, ladies usually tied scarves over their heads.

In 1936 actress and dancer Ginger Rogers sports sunglasses while relaxing on the beach. Rogers won the Academy Award for Best Actress in 1940.

DIAMONDS ARE A GIRL'S BEST FRIEND

Jewelry has long been a way for women to change the feel of an outfit. One unique 1930s style was the dress clip. Women clipped these decorations onto the necklines of their dresses, sometimes placing one clip on each side of a collar.

Late in the thirties, costume jewelry became more popular. Costume jewelry uses colored glass in place of diamonds, emeralds, and other precious gems. It also uses less expensive metals in place of gold and platinum.

Jewelry of the 1940s was often designed with sharp, geometric lines. The decade also saw a rise in novelty jewelry. These casual pieces were mass-produced and inexpensive. They came in fanciful shapes, such as animals, coins, swords, crowns, and shells. During World War II, novelty jewelry often featured U.S. flags and other patriotic themes.

A 1944 Sears catalog praised the virtues of the brooch. "With the final touch of beautiful jewelry, a woman's costume takes on individuality, compels attention and admiration." Matching sets, called parures, consisted of a necklace and a pair of earrings. Some sets also included a brooch.

Costume jewelry became ever more glamorous in the 1950s. Glimmering rhinestones (imitation diamonds) and Swarovski crystals gave the decade a decided sparkle.

SUNNY STYLES

Americans had begun wearing sunglasses in the late 1920s. They were practical as well as fashionable. Hollywood stars—living in the bright California sun—wore them to protect their eyes, and many other Americans followed suit. A 1939 article titled "How to Avoid the Summer Tragedy of Sun-Damaged Eyes" described sunglasses as style statements. "As Hollywood goes, so goes the fashion world. Luminaries [stars] like Joan Bennett . . . started the dark-glasses fad. Now it's an accepted style and health habit."

A rhinestone choker from a 1950s department store catalog

A teenage girl sports saddle shoes in 1937. These shoes—often in black and white—became very popular in the 1950s. Sometimes girls would wear a poodle skirt with saddle shoes.

blunt toes during the day. A dressier choice for afternoon or evening was the slingback. This shoe had a high or medium-height heel and featured a strap around the back of the ankle.

Casual footwear for women in the 1950s included saddle shoes. These low-heeled shoes were two-toned, usually white and black. The dark-colored section formed a saddle shape across the middle of the top of the foot. The style was particularly common among bobby-soxers. Dressy high-heeled shoes for nighttime were often covered in satin, decorated with bows or beads, or cut in stylish shapes.

Fancy Footwear

In the 1930s, two-tone shoes, introduced in the 1920s, were the peak of fashion for women. Some were low-heeled with a single strap across the top of the foot. Others were T-straps. A strap ran along the top of the foot and then met a strap that looped around the ankle, forming a *T*. By the late 1930s, many shoes featured ankle straps. Open-toed shoes also became fashionable in the thirties and remained a favorite style through the fifties.

The 1940s brought a fashion for ballet flats. Similar to the slippers worn by ballet dancers, the flat shoes had rounded toes and sometimes sported decorations such as bows. During the war, many women wore flats or sensible, low-heeled shoes with

A woman tries on a ballet flat adorned with a small bow in 1945. Ballet flats are still popular.

STICK YOUR
NECK OUT

Men also chose from a wide variety of accent items to complete their outfits. One of the most colorful men's accessories was the necktie. In the 1930s, men began wearing wide, bold ties. A Sears catalog at the end of the forties offered neckties sporting "distinctive patterns in a riot of brilliant colors." Many ties featured geometric patterns and combinations of elements such as swirls and diamonds. Others went even bolder, with novelty designs such as

- **horses**
- **fish**
- **palm trees**

In the early 1950s, ties were very wide. But late in the decade, ties became narrow and less tapered. For dressy occasions, men usually wore bow ties with tuxedos.

WATCH IT!

Before World War I (1914–1918), most men carried pocket watches. But by the beginning of the 1930s, pocket watches had fallen out of fashion. Veterans of WWI had gotten used to the practical wristwatches they had worn in combat. Until the late 1950s, wristwatches and pocket watches alike had complicated sets of interlocking gears. Winding a small knob on the outside of the watch set these gears in motion—but only temporarily. Watches had to be wound every day. In 1957 the first electric watches appeared, and being on time became easier than ever.

San Francisco mayor Roger Lapham shows off his necktie collection in the mid-1940s. He sports a tie with a bold print, which was very fashionable at the time.

GRAB YOUR COAT *and Get Your Hat*

To complete his look, a fashionable man needed the right overcoat. One classic choice from the 1930s through the 1950s was the trench coat. Double-breasted and belted, it was usually light tan in color. The garment's name reflects its military origins. Soldiers in World War I wore these coats in the trenches.

For dressier occasions, many men opted for the wool Chesterfield coat. This longer, tailored overcoat was somewhat fitted through the waist. Chesterfield coats could be single- or double-breasted. Traditionally, the Chesterfield was noted for its luxurious velvet collar.

In the 1950s, casual outerwear styles, known as loafer or leisure jackets, caught on. Some were waist-length with zippers and breast pockets. They were often made of sweaterlike knits and appeared in plaids and other patterns. Other leisure jackets were longer, buttoned up the front, and often had belts. The fifties also saw an increase in leather jackets. Edgier styles had an assortment of

- **zippers**
- **buckles**
- **rivets**
- **fur-trimmed collars** for a more conservative look

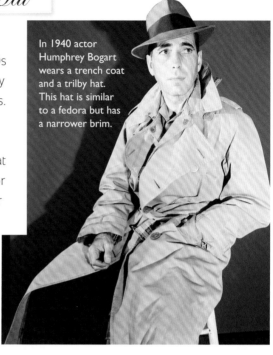

In 1940 actor Humphrey Bogart wears a trench coat and a trilby hat. This hat is similar to a fedora but has a narrower brim.

Coonskin caps were popular for boys in the 1950s.

FURRY FASHION

The 1950s brought a craze for coonskin caps among American boys. These hats are traditionally made of raccoon pelts, with the striped tail hanging down at the back. The fad really caught on in 1954, when actor Fess Parker played American frontier hero Davy Crockett in a popular Walt Disney TV series. Throughout the mid to late 1950s, boys all over the country sported the style. Many of the caps were actually made of fake fur.

In the early part of the twentieth century, a man rarely left home without a hat. (Etiquette, however, required him to take it off indoors.) In the 1930s, many men wore flat caps. These hats were low and flat, with narrow brims in front. They were soft, usually made of wool or felt. Some were knitted. While most were solid colors, some had patterns such as checks and plaids. Another 1930s style was the boater, also called a skimmer. Boaters are made of straw, and they have a stiff, flat brim and a low, flat crown. They often had white, black, or two-toned hatbands. Boaters were a popular choice for sailing outings.

The fedora had been widely popular among men since the 1920s. This brimmed hat is usually made of felt and comes in neutral colors. The fedora has a medium-height crown, with two indentations in the front and a lengthwise crease in the top. A fabric band runs around the base of the crown. By the 1940s, the fedora was everywhere. Movie stars—from tough-guy Humphrey Bogart to nice-guy Jimmy Stewart—wore fedoras in their films.

Panama hats (from Ecuador) also appeared often during this era. Panama hats are similar to fedoras but are made of straw. Many prominent men of the era favored Panama hats, including U.S. president Harry Truman.

A SHINE ON YOUR SHOES

In the late 1940s and the early 1950s, many men chose wing tip shoes. Their name comes from the vaguely winglike shape of the toe cap (a leather piece over the toes). Like most leather shoes, wing tips needed polishing to look sharp. Many U.S. cities had shoeshine booths on streets and in train stations. For a few cents, a man could get a fresh shine on his way to work.

Two-tone shoes—fashionable for women in the 1950s—were also popular with men. One common two-color style was the spectator shoe. Made of leather, it had a low heel and laces. Loafers were a more casual option in footwear in the 1950s. These slip-on leather shoes had no laces and were more comfortable than dressier shoes. They were popular among kids at prep schools and colleges. For swimming or other outdoorsy activities, some men chose sandals. The fifties also saw athletic shoes sneaking into everyday wear. Before that, men had only worn sneakers when they were exercising.

This man wears two-tone wing tip shoes in the 1940s. Another name for wing tip shoes is full brogues.

Chapter Five

DESIGNERS, PHOTOGRAPHERS, AND MODELS

Fashion designer Muriel King wears a gray and white flowered taffeta evening suit in 1946. King was one of the first well-known American designers.

One of the top American couturiers of the first half of the 1900s was Mainbocher. Born in Chicago, Illinois, in 1890 under the name Main Rousseau Bocher, he worked as a fashion illustrator at *Harper's Bazaar* and then as an editor for *Vogue*. In 1929, as Mainbocher, he founded his own fashion house in Paris, creating sophisticated and tasteful gowns. His career got a big boost in 1937, when Wallis Simpson chose him to design her wedding gown. Despite his success in Paris, Mainbocher returned to the United States in 1940 and set up shop in New York City.

The 1930s and the 1940s also saw an explosion of U.S. ready-to-wear fashion. New York City was home to innovative American designers such as Muriel King. Born in Bayview, Washington, in 1900, King produced simple but well-made designs that were popular with frugal Depression-era shoppers. Clare Potter, born in New Jersey in 1903, designed sportswear and separates in eye-catching color combinations.

First Lady Eleanor Roosevelt was one of Potter's customers.

Claire McCardell was another major American designer. Born in Frederick, Maryland, in 1905, she studied fashion in New York City and Paris. McCardell's approach to fashion was practical but chic. A 1955 *Time* magazine article described her as one of the makers of a new "American Look." McCardell created flattering, comfortable, ready-to-wear dresses that fit into the daily lives of many American women. Her 1942 Popover dress, for example, was an innovative, wide-sleeved wrap dress designed to go over other, dressier clothes. The ensemble was suitable for doing work, while still looking stylish. Another casually chic McCardell look was a 1956 plaid sundress with a halter-style neck.

Eleanor Roosevelt *(left)* wears a look created by Clare Potter while talking with Queen Elizabeth *(right)* in 1942.

These models display 1946 summer outfits by Claire McCardell. McCardell was known for her ready-to-wear clothing.

" **I'VE ALWAYS** DESIGNED THINGS I NEED MYSELF. **IT JUST TURNS OUT THAT OTHER PEOPLE** NEED THEM, TOO. "

—Claire McCardell, American fashion designer, 1955

Bonnie Cashin was another American designer of the 1950s. She created inexpensive ready-made garments as well as haute couture looks.

Meanwhile, Europe remained a center of high fashion that influenced the way Europeans and Americans dressed. In addition to top names such as Chanel, Schiaparelli, and Dior, a number of other European designers made their mark. Emilio Pucci of Italy came to fashion fame in an unusual way. Pucci loved designing ski outfits. In 1947 a friend of Pucci's wore one of these outfits during a Swiss skiing holiday. The splashy garment caught the eye of Tony Frissell, a fashion photographer for *Harper's Bazaar* magazine. Frissell's photos earned Pucci publicity as well as clients. Pucci went on to create a wide variety of sportswear and swimwear, making good use of new stretchy fabrics. He soon expanded his line beyond sportswear, making blouses and dresses in colorful prints.

British designer Edward Molyneux, born in London in 1891, began his fashion career as an illustrator. Like so many aspiring designers, he pursued his dreams in Paris and opened a fashion house there in 1919.

Fashion designer Molyneux was known for his graceful looks, like this 1931 long white beaded dress with a rhinestone buckle belt.

His looks were simple, elegant, and tasteful. He combined muted colors and clean, crisp lines with occasional flourishes, such as a daringly low back on a stunning white evening gown.

Spanish designer Cristóbal Balenciaga was born in 1895 in Guetaria, a fishing village on Spain's northern coast. His mother was a dressmaker, and when Balenciaga was a child, he often watched her work. When he was about twelve, he became a tailor's apprentice. As a teenager, he made a trip to Paris that inspired him to pursue a fashion career. He opened his first shop in San Sebastián—a resort town in northern Spain—in 1914. He later relocated to Paris, founding his high-fashion house there in 1937. Balenciaga created dramatic, sculptural clothes.

Hubert de Givenchy was a couturier from northern France. His wealthy and well-connected family helped him land his first job in fashion, working for designer Jacques Fath. In 1952 Givenchy opened his own house in Paris. Givenchy's clothes were glamorous without being flashy, and they appealed to a sophisticated, elegant clientele. In 1954 he expanded his business to include a ready-to-wear line.

This model wears a luxurious 1939 Balenciaga design—a scarlet satin coat with panniers over a hooped gown of black lace. Panniers expand the width of a skirt at the sides.

PICTURE PERFECT

Fashion shows are an important part of getting the word out about the latest fashions. At the same time, fashion shows help designers find customers. But only a small, select group of people see these shows. To reach a broader audience, designers rely on advertisements and fashion magazines. That's where fashion photographers enter the picture.

The 1930s through the 1950s were great decades for fashion photography. Among the many talented photographers of the time was Horst P. Horst. Born in 1906 in eastern Germany, he began working for *Vogue* in 1931. One of Horst's most famous images is a 1939 shot of a model wearing a white, lace-up corset designed by Mainbocher. The photo seems to capture a woman in the process of dressing—or perhaps undressing. Considered risqué at the time, the Mainbocher Corset has become an iconic image of classic fashion.

Two American women made their mark on fashion photography during the era. **Frances McLaughlin-Gill**, born in 1919, worked for Condé Nast, a group that manages many publications. In the 1940s, she became the first female photographer with a contract to work for *Vogue*. She was known for her good relationship with models, making her photos feel remarkably natural. Another noted female fashion photographer of the time was **Lillian Bassman**. Born in New York in 1917, she worked for *Harper's Bazaar* for decades. Bassman became known for her striking black-and-white, high-contrast images. She also often used unusual angles and sharp geometric shapes in her shots.

Richard Avedon was born in New York City in 1923. His career in photography began early, starting when he was just nineteen years old and taking pictures for the military in World War II. He went on to become one of the greatest fashion and portrait photographers in history. He worked for some of the biggest publications in the industry, including *Harper's Bazaar*, *Vogue*, and *Life* magazines.

Other major photographers of the time period include **Georges Dambier, George Hoyningen-Huene, Erwin Blumenfeld, Irving Penn, and Gordon Parks**. Parks, in particular, was a trailblazer. In the mid-1940s, when racial discrimination and segregation were still widespread, he was one of the first African American photographers to work for *Vogue*.

MODISH MEDIA

The media is a key part of the fashion industry. Fashion magazines report on new styles, publish the work of talented photographers, and champion young designers.

When the 1930s began, *Vogue* magazine had already been fashion journalism's gold standard for decades. *Vogue* was founded in 1892, and modern observers regard it as the biggest influence in the fashion business. But a host of other publications have also reported on fashion over the years. *Harper's Bazaar* hit newsstands in 1867 and was notable as the first fashion magazine to come from U.S. publishers. *Women's Wear Daily* began in 1910. While it didn't gain the same highbrow reputation as *Vogue*, it was widely popular by the 1950s. *Esquire*—a men's magazine that began in 1932—is important as one of the few publications covering men's fashions and other style-related topics. Another U.S. fashion magazine, *Seventeen*, was founded in 1944. At that time, it was unique for its focus on young people and their styles.

This 1939 image for *Vogue* of a model wearing a corset designed by Mainbocher is one of Horst P. Horst's most famous fashion photographs.

Model Behavior

Models are key to the success of fashion. Some walk the runway, wearing haute couture gowns in front of live audiences. Others specialize in modeling for high-fashion photos. Still others work with commercial and ready-to-wear companies such as Sears.

One American family boasted two top models. Dorian Leigh and her sister Suzy Parker were born in Texas in 1917 and 1933, respectively. Despite her father's protests, Leigh became a model and rocketed to fame.

Between 1946 and 1952, more than fifty magazine covers featured her image. She appeared on the cover of *Vogue* seven times in 1946 alone. She worked with many of the best photographers in the business, including Cecil Beaton and Irving Penn. Penn described working with Leigh: "She seems to sense the coming click of the camera; her expression builds until she and the camera come alive together."

Suzy Parker became a model with the help of her successful sister. Parker worked closely with Chanel and became one of the most highly paid models of the era, earning up to two hundred dollars an hour. Both Leigh and Parker modeled for cosmetics companies, especially Revlon.

Model Suzy Parker wears a Givenchy look consisting of a black lace petticoat, a swinging lacquer-printed skirt, and a quilted satin jacket in 1953. Parker started modeling after her sister Dorian Leigh became a famous model.

Dorian Leigh models a jacket design by Traina-Norell in 1950. Leigh was short for a model, standing at five feet five inches tall.

FASHION ON FILM

Audrey Hepburn was a muse to Hubert de Givenchy. During the 1950s and the 1960s, she also inspired fashion photographer Richard Avedon. Avedon said, "I am, and forever will be, devastated by the gift of Audrey Hepburn before my camera."

Hepburn's 1957 film *Funny Face* is loosely based on Avedon's career. Actor, singer, and dancer Fred Astaire plays fashion photographer Dick Avery, who stumbles upon Audrey Hepburn's character, Jo Stockton. Stockton is a young, intellectual, and slightly mousy bookshop worker. Recognizing her as a diamond in the rough, Avery transforms her into a high-fashion model.

Just as Avedon inspired Avery's character, Stockton is roughly based on model Suzy Parker. The real-life Parker makes a brief appearance in the film. In addition, Dovima plays a humorous role as a gorgeous but rather dimwitted model.

The action is set against the always-fashionable backdrops of New York City and Paris, and Hepburn wears a stunning wardrobe by Givenchy. The film endures as a love letter to the world of fashion.

Audrey Hepburn (wearing Givenchy) in the 1957 film *Funny Face*

Another top model came from the U.S. fashion capital of New York City. The model famous as Dovima was born in 1927 as Dorothy Virginia Margaret Juba. After a *Vogue* editor spotted her on a Manhattan street, she quickly became one of the fifties' most popular models. Dovima's dark hair, sharp cheekbones, and arched eyebrows made hers a face to remember. She worked with Richard Avedon and Irving Penn on dramatic, artistic shoots. Dovima left modeling behind in 1962. The reason she gave was simple: "I didn't want to wait until the camera turned cruel."

Other popular models of the era included Sunny Harnett and Jean Patchett. In addition, film stars often took the place of professional models. The French designer Givenchy found great inspiration in the actress Audrey Hepburn, whom he met in 1953. He quickly recognized Audrey's beauty as well as her impeccable style. Hepburn went on to wear Givenchy clothes, designed especially for her, in films and fashion shoots.

In this 1953 photo, movie star Marilyn Monroe wears one of her famous outfits—a gold lamé gown created by Bill Travilla for the 1953 movie *Gentlemen Prefer Blondes*. The images of movie stars like Monroe are just as enchanting these days as they were in the 1950s.

EPILOGUE

The thirties, the forties, and the fifties were momentous decades in American history—and in American fashion. The tough years of the Depression had forced people to get by with less luxurious clothes. At the same time, stars of the silver screen became greater fashion icons than ever before. This combination of hardship and glamour largely defined the 1930s. During the war years of the 1940s, a make-do attitude on the home front, combined with innovative designers, brought the United States new recognition in the fashion world. And with the postwar boom came an era of prosperity and a return to optimism. From the dinner pajama to the New Look to blue jeans and black leather jackets, the era featured unforgettable styles.

The growing influence of young people on fashion in the 1950s would only become stronger in the 1960s. The decade earned the nickname the Swinging Sixties, hinting at the energy and free spirits of the times. London, in particular, became a hotbed of new, edgy fashion. Hemlines crept higher than ever before. Music and politics affected fashion more directly than in the past. A person's clothing was often a political or social statement, reflecting aspects of his or her personality and beliefs. A new youth-oriented counterculture group emerged during the 1960s. Known as hippies, they embraced peace, love, and a live-and-let-live philosophy. Their fashions were equally easygoing. Long gone were the tailored suits of the 1940s and prim twin sets of the 1950s.

"FASHION PASSES STYLE REMAINS."

—Coco Chanel,
French fashion designer, n.d.

Such dramatic shifts are not unusual. In fashion, three decades may as well be several lifetimes. Trends are ever-changing and moods swing quickly. For instance, loose, untailored dresses had been the height of sophistication in the 1920s. But just ten years later, *Time* magazine wrote disdainfully of "the hideous, bag-shaped style . . . when the flour-sack dress flourished and the straight line conquered all." Similarly, the various fashions that flourished in the thirties, the forties, and the fifties swiftly disappeared as the looks of the sixties took to the runways and the streets. But many fashion historians and lovers of vintage style consider this era a classic one. Part of this ongoing popularity stems from the fact that filmgoers still watch, admire, and love the movies of the time. In fact, the years between the late 1920s and the late 1950s are often called the Golden Age of Hollywood. Images of Marlene Dietrich,

Greta Garbo, Audrey Hepburn, and Marilyn Monroe in their sensational gowns are just as glamorous in the twenty-first century as they were when they first appeared. James Dean and Marlon Brando have an enduring cool that still radiates off the screen.

Fashion can often be strange, silly, and over-the-top. No matter what, it captures the spirit of its times. The thirty years between 1930 and 1959 are no exception. The styles from the Depression to the postwar boom present a vivid snapshot of the United States in a time of unique challenges and change.

Hippies of the 1960s wore carefree fashions such as this colorful floral print and leather headband. Hippies promoted peace and love.

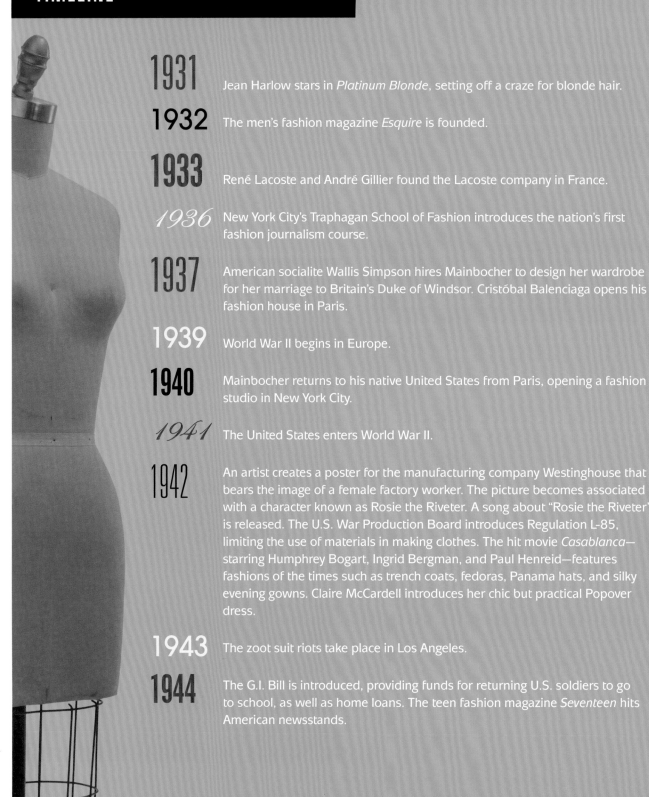

TIMELINE

1931 Jean Harlow stars in *Platinum Blonde*, setting off a craze for blonde hair.

1932 The men's fashion magazine *Esquire* is founded.

1933 René Lacoste and André Gillier found the Lacoste company in France.

1936 New York City's Traphagan School of Fashion introduces the nation's first fashion journalism course.

1937 American socialite Wallis Simpson hires Mainbocher to design her wardrobe for her marriage to Britain's Duke of Windsor. Cristóbal Balenciaga opens his fashion house in Paris.

1939 World War II begins in Europe.

1940 Mainbocher returns to his native United States from Paris, opening a fashion studio in New York City.

1941 The United States enters World War II.

1942 An artist creates a poster for the manufacturing company Westinghouse that bears the image of a female factory worker. The picture becomes associated with a character known as Rosie the Riveter. A song about "Rosie the Riveter" is released. The U.S. War Production Board introduces Regulation L-85, limiting the use of materials in making clothes. The hit movie *Casablanca*—starring Humphrey Bogart, Ingrid Bergman, and Paul Henreid—features fashions of the times such as trench coats, fedoras, Panama hats, and silky evening gowns. Claire McCardell introduces her chic but practical Popover dress.

1943 The zoot suit riots take place in Los Angeles.

1944 The G.I. Bill is introduced, providing funds for returning U.S. soldiers to go to school, as well as home loans. The teen fashion magazine *Seventeen* hits American newsstands.

1945 World War II ends.

1946 French designer Jacques Heim and French engineer Louis Réard both introduce tiny two-piece bathing suits. The controversial swimwear becomes known worldwide as the bikini. American model Dorian Leigh appears on the cover of *Vogue* seven times.

1947 French designer Christian Dior introduces the fashion line that comes to be known as the New Look. Emilio Pucci gets noticed for his fashionable skiing attire. He will go on to launch a popular line of sportswear.

1951 The popular television sitcom *I Love Lucy* begins airing. American women take style cues from Lucille Ball and other TV stars.

1952 Hubert de Givenchy opens his Parisian fashion house.

1953 Marlon Brando stars in *The Wild One*. His rebellious jeans-and-leather-jacket look inspires many young male dressers. Elsa Schiaparelli releases a small line of menswear. French fashion designer Hubert de Givenchy meets American film star Audrey Hepburn. She goes on to become his muse.

1954 Coco Chanel reopens her fashion studio (after closing it during World War II) in Paris. Chanel's sometime rival Elsa Schiaparelli closes her house. Fess Parker wears a coonskin cap in a Disney TV miniseries about Davy Crockett, inspiring a craze for the hats.

1955 James Dean stars in *Rebel Without a Cause*. Dean's style inspires many young American men. Model Dovima and photographer Richard Avedon create an enduring fashion image, "Dovima with Elephants."

1957 Christian Dior dies suddenly, and Yves Saint Laurent takes over the Dior house. Cristóbal Balenciaga introduces his sack dress. Pierre Cardin opens a menswear store in Paris. Electric wristwatches are introduced. The film *Funny Face*, starring Audrey Hepburn and Fred Astaire, takes a lighthearted look into the fashion world.

1958 Saint Laurent presents his first collection as head of Dior, featuring his Trapeze line.

1959 British designer Hardy Amies produces a menswear line. Italian shoe designer Salvatore Ferragamo makes a pair of red-crystal-encrusted high heels for movie megastar Marilyn Monroe.

GLOSSARY

beret: a soft, round cap of French design and usually made of felt. Berets were popular in the United States throughout the 1930s.

bespoke: made to order, usually referring to clothing such as men's suits

bikini: a very small, two-piece swimsuit for women introduced in France in 1946. Unlike earlier, more modest two-piece suits, the bikini revealed the belly button.

bleach: to remove the color from something. Inspired by film star Jean Harlow, many women bleached their hair blonde or even white in the 1930s.

boater: a men's straw hat with a flat top and brim. Sometimes boaters are also called skimmers. They were popular in the 1930s.

bobby-soxer: a teenage girl of the 1950s. The term originally referred to fans of singer Frank Sinatra but later to a group of teenage girls. Many bobby-soxers wore short white socks, poodle skirts, and sweaters or buttoned shirts.

bolero: a short, open women's jacket that ends above the waist and that is based on Spanish bullfighter jackets. Boleros became fashionable outerwear in the 1950s.

Chesterfield coat: a tailored men's overcoat, traditionally having a velvet collar. Chesterfields were popular throughout the thirties, the forties, and the fifties.

chignon: an elegant women's hairstyle, comprised of a simple bun set on the back of the head (either high or low) and held in place with pins or other fasteners. Chignons were very fashionable in the 1950s.

corset: an undergarment for women that shapes the bust and waist through tight lacing and a set of bone or steel rods

couturier: an haute couture (high-fashion) designer

double-breasted suit: a men's suit that has two vertical rows of buttons in the front to close the suit. Suits with a single row of buttons are called single-breasted.

ducktail: a slicked-back men's hairstyle featuring a tapered neckline. Men often used pomade (a hair product) to keep the style in place. The ducktail was a fashionable style in the 1950s.

fedora: a men's hat made of felt and featuring a slightly curled brim and a creased crown. Fedoras were hugely popular from the 1930s through the 1950s.

haute couture: high-quality fashion design. *Haute couture* means "high dressmaking" or "high sewing" in French.

New Look: the name for a fashion line that French designer Christian Dior introduced in 1947. It emphasized an exaggerated feminine silhouette, with curvy busts, tiny waists, and very full skirts.

nylon: a strong but lightweight synthetic (man-made) fabric

pageboy: a chin-length women's hairstyle featuring hair curled under at the ends and sometimes including short bangs. Pageboys were popular in the fifties.

pompadour: a men's hairstyle popular in the 1950s. The pompadour features hair combed upward from the forehead, without a part, and is held in place with pomade or other hair products.

poodle skirt: a full, usually colorful felt skirt featuring an image of a poodle sewed onto the skirt. Bobby-soxers of the 1950s often wore poodle skirts.

ration: to limit certain goods, often because there is a shortage

smoking jacket: a men's belted jacket designed for at-home leisure or entertaining. In the 1950s, men traditionally wore silk or velvet smoking jackets while smoking tobacco after dinner.

sport coat: a men's tailored jacket, similar to a suit coat but without a matching pair of trousers. Sport coats became popular in the 1950s.

surrealism: an artistic movement that began in Paris in the 1920s and flourished in the 1930s. Surrealists attempted to reach their creative potential by combining unexpected images and ideas. Elsa Schiaparelli combined surrealism and high fashion in her famous lobster dress, a relatively simple white gown with a large lobster hand painted by surrealist artist Salvador Dalí on the skirt.

trench coat: a durable, double-breasted, belted raincoat that became popular in the 1940s. The coat was based on those that U.S. soldiers wore during World War I.

twin set: a 1950s look for women, consisting of a well-fitted cardigan sweater over a matching short-sleeved top

vogue: the fashion, or style, of a certain time. When something is in fashion, it is said to be in vogue.

SOURCE NOTES

4   Stella Blum, ed., *Everyday Fashions of the Thirties as Pictured in Sears Catalogs* (New York: Dover Publications, 1986), v.

4   Ibid.

6   JoAnne Olian, ed., *Everyday Fashions of the Forties as Pictured in Sears Catalogs* (New York: Dover Publications, 1992), iii.

6   Harris, *Vintage Fashions for Women*, 102.

7   Blum, *Everyday Fashions of the Thirties*, 71.

8   Kristina Harris, *Vintage Fashions for Women: 1920s–1940s* (Atglen, PA: Schiffer Publishing, 1996), 104.

8   Blum, *Everyday Fashions of the Thirties*, 20.

9   Doris Kearns Goodwin, *No Ordinary Time: Franklin and Eleanor Roosevelt: The Home Front in World War II* (New York: Simon & Schuster, 1994), 414.

10   Jonathan Walford, *Forties Fashion: From Siren Suits to the New Look* (New York: Thames and Hudson, 2008), 94.

10   Ibid., 127.

11   Elizabeth D. Hoover, "60 Years of Bikinis," AmericanHeritage.com, 2008, http://www.americanheritage.com/articles/web/20060705-bikini-swimming-suit-louis-reard-micheline-bernardini-paris-brigitte-bardot.shtml (February 14, 2011).

13   Linda Watson, *20th Century Fashion: 100 Years of Style by Decade and Designer, in Association with* Vogue (Buffalo: Firefly Books, 2004), 83.

15   Elsa Schiaparelli, as told to Harold S. Kahn, *Photoplay Magazine*, "How to be Chic on a Small Income," August 1936, http://www.oldmagazinearticles.com/pdf/Schiaparelli-article.pdf (March 8, 2011).

16   Watson, 20th Century Fashion, 64.

17   Ibid., 70.

17   Daniel Delis Hill, *As Seen in Vogue: A Century of American Fashion in Advertising* (Lubbock: Texas Tech University Press, 2004), 67.

17   Olian, *Everyday Fashions of the Forties*, 86.

17   Hill, *As Seen in Vogue*, 75.

18   Ibid., 76.

18   Christian Dior, *The Little Dictionary of Fashion: A Guide to Dress Sense for Every Woman* (New York: Abrams, 2007), 5.

18   Watson, *20th Century Fashion*, 74.

19   *Time*, "The Word Is Chemise," February 10, 1958, http://www.time.com/time/magazine/article/0,9171,868281,00.html (February 14, 2011).

19   Ibid.

20   Hill, *As Seen in Vogue*, 84.

23   Blum, *Everyday Fashions of the Thirties*, 35.

27   *Time*, "Women's Clothes: Why Are They So Expensive?" August 31, 1953, http://www.time.com/time/magazine/article/0,9171,823020,00.html (February 14, 2011).

36   Watson, *20th Century Fashion*, 81.

37   Watson, *20th Century Fashion*, 56.

38   Blum, *Everyday Fashions of the Thirties*, 54.

39   Roseann Ettinger, *40s and 50s Popular Jewelry* (Atglen, PA: Schiffer Publishing, 2003), 10.

39   *Click National Picture Monthly*, "How to Avoid the Summer Tragedy of Sun-Damaged Eyes," July 1939, http://www.oldmagazinearticles.com/pdf/Sun-glasses-1939.pdf (February 14, 2011).

41   Olian, *Everyday Fashions of the Forties*, 116.

45   *Time*, "The American Look," May 2, 1955, http://www.time.com/time/magazine/article/0,9171,866314,00.html (February 14, 2011).

50   Cathy Horyn, "Perhaps More Than Just Pretty Faces," *New York Times*, May 5, 2009, http://www.nytimes.com/2009/05/06/arts/design/06mode.html (February 14, 2011).

51 Bernadine Morris, "Dovima, a Regal Model of the 50's, Is Dead at 63," *New York Times*, May 5, 1990, http://www.nytimes .com/1990/05/05/obituaries/dovima-a-regal-model-of-the-50-s-is-dead-at-63.html (February 14, 2011).

51 Robyn Karney, *Audrey Hepburn: A Star Danced* (New York: Arcade Publishing, 1995), 8.

53 *Time*, "Waistline Extended," March 11, 1940, http://www.time.com/time/magazine/ article/0,9171,789652,00.html (February 14, 2011).

53 Julia Neel, "Mademoiselle Coco Speaks," Vogue.com, July 17, 2009, http://www.vogue .co.uk/celebrity-photos/090717-coco-chanel-quotes-and-photos.aspx (March 8, 2011).

SELECTED BIBLIOGRAPHY

Blum, Stella, ed. *Everyday Fashions of the Thirties as Pictured in Sears Catalogs*. New York: Dover Publications, 1986.

Crane, Diana. *Fashion and Its Social Agendas: Class, Gender, and Identity in Clothing*. Chicago: University of Chicago Press, 2000.

Dior, Christian. *The Little Dictionary of Fashion: A Guide to Dress Sense for Every Woman*. New York: Abrams, 2007.

Ettinger, Roseann. *50s Popular Fashions for Men, Women, Boys, and Girls*. Atglen, PA: Schiffer Publishing, 1995.

Harris, Kristina. *Vintage Fashions for Women: 1920s–1940s*. Atglen, PA: Schiffer Publishing, 1996.

———. *Vintage Fashions for Women: The 1950s and 60s*. Atglen, PA: Schiffer Publishing, 1997.

Hill, Daniel Delis. *As Seen in Vogue: A Century of American Fashion in Advertising*. Lubbock: Texas Tech University Press, 2004.

Hunt, Marsha. *The Way We Wore: Styles of the 1930s and '40s and Our World Since Then*. Fallbrook, CA: Fallbrook Publishing, 1992.

Joselit, Jenna Weissman. *A Perfect Fit: Clothes, Character, and the Promise of America*. New York: Henry Holt and Company, 2001.

Mendes, Valerie D. *Fashion since 1900*. New York: Thames and Hudson, 2010.

Murray, Maggie Pexton. *Changing Styles in Fashion: Who, What, Why*. New York: Fairchild Publications, 1989.

Olian, JoAnne, ed. *Everyday Fashions of the Forties as Pictured in Sears Catalogs*. New York: Dover Publications, 1992.

Peacock, John. *Fashions since 1900: The Complete Sourcebook*. New York: Thames and Hudson, 2007.

Pochna, Marie-France. Translated by Joanna Savill. *Christian Dior: The Man Who Made the World Look New*. New York: Arcade Publishing, 1996.

Rubinstein, Ruth P. *Dress Codes: Meanings and Messages in American Culture*. Boulder, CO: Westview Press, 1995.

Smith, Desire. *Fashionable Clothing from the Sears Catalogs: Early 1950s*. Atglen, PA: Schiffer Publishing, 1998.

———. *Vintage Style: 1920–1960*. Atglen, PA: Schiffer Publishing, 1997.

Stanton, Shelby. *U.S. Army Uniforms of World War II*. Harrisburg, PA: Stackpole Books, 1991.

Walford, Jonathan. *Forties Fashion: From Siren Suits to the New Look*. New York: Thames and Hudson, 2008.

Watson, Linda. *20th Century Fashion: 100 Years of Style by Decade and Designer, in Association with Vogue*. Buffalo: Firefly Books, 2004.

FURTHER READING, WEBSITES, AND FILMS

BOOKS

Beker, Jeanne. *Passion for Fashion: Careers in Style*. Toronto: Tundra Books, 2008.
If you have a passion for fashion, let Jeanne Beker—a fashion writer and actress—tell you about ways you can make it your career.

Damon, Duane. *Headin' for Better Times: The Arts of the Great Depression*. Minneapolis: Twenty-First Century Books, 2002.
Fashion wasn't the only form of artistic expression that changed and grew during the troubled 1930s. This book explores other American art from the Depression years.

Gaines, Ann. *Coco Chanel*. Philadelphia: Chelsea House, 2004.
Chanel was among the most important designers of her era. Find out more about her life in this biography.

Lindop, Edmund, and Margaret J. Goldstein. *America in the 1930s*. Minneapolis: Twenty-First Century Books, 2010.
Learn more about the lives and times of Americans during this decade. The same series (The Decades of Twentieth-Century America) also includes titles on the 1940s and the 1950s.

MacDonald, Fiona. *Everyday Clothes through History*. Milwaukee: G. Stevens Publishers, 2007.
Learn more about what kinds of clothes people have worn over the years and why.

Marcovitz, Hal. *Surrealism*. Detroit: Lucent Books, 2008.
Explore the artistic movement that so inspired Elsa Schiaparelli and other designers of the times.

Sills, Leslie. *From Rags to Riches: A History of Girls' Clothing in America*. New York: Holiday House, 2005.
Take a look at how styles have changed for girls in the United States over the years.

WEBSITES

The Bata Shoe Museum
http://www.batashoemuseum.ca
This museum, based in Toronto, Canada, holds thousands of shoes from all over the world and all time periods. Its website offers a glimpse of this amazing collection.

The Fashion Encyclopedia
http://www.fashionencyclopedia.com/
This online resource features articles on the major designers of the 1930s through the 1950s, including images of the designers' work. The site also presents articles on the fashions of various time periods.

NewsHour Extra: Yves Saint Laurent, Fashion Designer
http://www.pbs.org/newshour/extra/features/jan-june02/yves.html
Find out more about Yves Saint Laurent's long and groundbreaking career at this PBS-run page.

Shocking! The Art and Fashion of Elsa Schiaparelli
http://www.philamuseum.org/micro_sites/exhibitions/schiaparelli/home.htm
This site from the Philadelphia Museum of Art takes visitors inside the fascinating world of Elsa Schiaparelli's designs.

Style Blog
http://www.seventeen.com/fashion/blog/
From *Seventeen* magazine, this blog for young fashion lovers offers style advice, shopping tips, and more.

Style Rookie
http://www.thestylerookie.com/
Teenaged fashionista Tavi Gevinson began this fashion blog in 2008—at the age of eleven—and has become one of the style world's freshest voices.

Teen Vogue
http://www.teenvogue.com
The famous fashion magazine *Vogue* has a special publication just for teens. Check out the website for news and information on designers and trends.

Victoria and Albert Museum: Fashion, Jewelry, and Accessories
http://www.vam.ac.uk/collections/fashion/index.html
This museum in London, England, boasts a large collection of clothes and other fashionable items. Get a glimpse of this collection by browsing the website.

FILMS

Funny Face. DVD. Hollywood CA: Paramount Pictures, 1957.
This classic musical, starring Audrey Hepburn and Fred Astaire, is most fashionable, featuring clothes by Hubert de Givenchy as well as costumes by American designer Edith Head.

The September Issue. DVD. New York: A&E Indie Films, 2009.
Vogue magazine is the world's most influential fashion publication and has been for decades. This recent documentary takes viewers behind the scenes.

Yves St. Laurent: His Life and Times. DVD. Paris: Movimento Productions, 2002.
This documentary (in French, with English subtitles) explores the life and career of designer Saint Laurent, who took over the fashion house of Dior as a young man in 1957.

 LERNER e SOURCE
Expand learning beyond the printed book. Download free, complementary educational resources for this book from our website, www.lerneresource.com.

INDEX

ABOUT THE AUTHOR

Alison Marie Behnke is a book editor and author working in Minneapolis, Minnesota. Among her many books are *Italy in Pictures*, *Does a Ten-Gallon Hat Really Hold Ten Gallons? And Other Questions about Fashion*, and *Jack Kerouac*. She spent several years living in Rome, Italy, where she gained a greater appreciation than ever for fashion. One of her style icons is Audrey Hepburn.

PHOTO ACKNOWLEDGMENTS

The images in this book are used with the permission of: © Jameswimsel/Dreamstime.com, pp. 1, 54; © George Karger/Pix Inc./Time Life Pictures/Getty Images, p. 3; © Sasha/Hutlon Archive/Getty Images, p. 4; © Scotty Welbourne/Contributor/Hulton Archive/Getty Images, p. 5; Advertising Archive/Courtesy Everett Collection, p. 6; © Photo by Kenneth Alexander/John Kobal Foundation/Getty Images, p. 7; © H. Armstrong Roberts/ClassicStock/The Image Works, p. 8 (top); © Horace Eliascheff/Hulton Archive/Getty Images, p. 8 (bottom); National Archives, p. 9; © Make and Mend, 1942/Independent Picture Service, p. 10; © H. Armstrong Roberts/ClassicStock/Alamy, p. 11; © Sharland/Time Life Pictures/Getty Images, p. 12 (left); © Camerique/ClassicStock/CORBIS, p. 12 (right); © CORBIS, p. 13 (top); © SuperStock, p. 13 (bottom); © Philadelphia Museum of Art/Art Resource, NY, p. 14; © Bettman/CORBIS, p. 15; © Sunset Boulevard/CORBIS, p. 16; Photo by Rex Features/Everett Collection, p. 17; AP Photo, pp. 18, 19; © Bettman/CORBIS, pp. 20, 23, 25; © Keystone/Stringer/Hulton Archive/Getty Images, p. 21; © Alfred Eisenstaedt/Time & Life Pictures/Getty Images, pp. 22, 34 (top), 40 (top); © Lambert/Contributor/Archive Photos/Getty Images, p. 24; © George Skadding/Contributor/Time & Life Pictures/Getty Images, p. 26; © George Marks/Stringer/Retrofile/Getty Images, p. 27; Columbia/The Kobal Collection, p. 28; © Image Of Our Lives/Archive Photos/Getty Images, p. 29 (top); © Norma Zuniga/Stone/Getty Images, p. 29 (bottom); © Hulton Archive/Stringer/Getty Images, pp. 30, 35; © Universal/TempSport/CORBIS, p. 31; © John Springer Collection/CORBIS, p. 32; © George Hurrell/John Kobal Foundation/Getty Images, p. 33; © Silver Screen Collection/Archive Photos/Getty Images, p. 34 (bottom); © Michael Ochs Archives/Stringer/Getty Images, p. 36 (Left); © Carl Iwasaki/Contributor/Time & Life Pictures/Getty Images, p. 36 (right); © George Marks/Stringer/Retrofile/Getty Images, p. 37; © Chaloner Woods/Getty Images, p. 38 (left); © Clarence Sinclair Bull/John Kobal Foundation/Getty Images, p. 38 (right); © John Kobal Foundation/Hulton Archive/Getty Images, pp. 39 (top), 42 (top); © PoodlesRock/CORBIS, p. 39 (bottom); © Jerry Cooke/Contributor/Time & Life Pictures/Getty Images, p. 40 (bottom); © Ralph Crane/Time Life Pictures/Getty Images, p. 41; © John Dominis/Time Life Pictures/Getty Images, p. 42 (bottom); H. Armstrong Roberts/ClassicStock/Everett Collection, p. 43; © Constantin Joffe/Condé Nast Archive/CORBIS, p. 44; Franklin D. Roosevelt Presidential Library, p. 45 (top); © Genevieve Naylor/CORBIS, p. 45 (bottom); © Edward Steichen/Conde Nast/CORBIS, p. 46; © Agenta Fischer/Hulton Archive/Getty Images, p. 47; © CNAC/MNAM/Dist. Réunion des Musées Nationaux/Art Resource, NY, p. 49; © John Rawlings/Condé Nast Archive/CORBIS, p. 50 (left); © Gjon Mili/Time Life Pictures/Getty Images, p. 50 (right); Everett Collection, p. 51; © Ed Clark/Time & Life Pictures/Getty Images, p. 52; © Henry Diltz/Encyclopedia/CORBIS, p. 53.

Front Cover © Silver Screen Collection/Hulton Archive/Getty Images.
Back cover: © Photofest.

Main body text provided by Mixage ITC Book 10/15
Typeface provided by International Typeface Corp